ACCE

NORFOLK
Constabulary

"Serving the community"

Let's Go Out

A ROAD SAFETY ACTIVITY BOOK FOR PARENTS AND YOUNG CHILDREN

LONDON: HMSO

© Crown Copyright 1991
Applications for reproduction should be made to HMSO
First Published 1991
ISBN 011 550993 3

Produced by Complete Editions
Written by Jan Gridley-Sigsworth
Designed and illustrated by David Mostyn

British Library Cataloguing in Publication Data

A CIP catalogue record for this book is available from the British Library

Foreword

Mr P Ryan M.Sc, B.A, D.M.S., F.B.I.M..
CHIEF CONSTABLE
Norfolk Constabulary

Teaching road safety to one's children is amongst the most important duties of a parent. As a father of two young children, I am frequently distressed to hear of the many road accidents involving young people which could have been prevented had simple road safety advice been followed.

In an effort to reduce road accidents, this book, *Let's Go Out* has been produced, which in an interesting and informative way will help you to teach your children to become safer and less vulnerable to other road users.

Covering all aspects of road safety *Let's Go Out* involves children in the learning process by combining play, questions and guidance in a way which helps to develop a knowledge of how to stay safe.

I hope that you and your children enjoy using Lets Go Out and please remember, "STAY SAFE".

I would like to dedicate this book to my two sons Adam and Ben Sigsworth.

I would also like to acknowledge the help and support I have received from Mary Tyler and Dave Taylor MBE, the Traffic Education campaigner.

Jan Gridley-Sigsworth

HMSO gratefully acknowledges the assistance given by the Community Relations Branch of the Norfolk Constabulary and Norfolk County Council's Road Safety Section in the preparation of this book.

Contents

Introduction

One quarter of all British schoolchildren who die are killed in road accidents and one in fifteen British children can expect to be injured in a road accident before their sixteenth birthday.

Let's do what we can to ensure your children aren't among them.

As individuals there's little we can do about the volume of traffic or standards of driving on our roads. We can't cocoon our children from the realities – and the dangers – of the modern world. But we can make them safer by teaching them about traffic hazards and, from a young age, gradually instilling in them the fundamentals of road safety. This book aims to make the learning process interesting and fun for both adults and children. As well as highlighting the obvious (and not-so-obvious) dangers, it is packed with ideas for activities, games and projects which you can enjoy doing together.

From children's first awareness of roads and traffic, it takes them stage by stage through the basic training as pedestrians to the point when they can learn and understand the Green Cross Code, somewhere between the ages of seven and nine. The book also covers the crucial facts behind protecting children as passengers. It does not, however, attempt to cover cycling on the road, which should only be undertaken by children aged nine or over, and only then after careful training and preparation. *Keep on the Safe Side* (also published by HMSO) is an ideal handbook for young cyclists.

As adults, even as adults caring for the under-fives, we tend to assume that young children see the world in much the same way as we do. We forget that children cannot judge speed or distance accurately, that they cannot concentrate on more than one thing at a time and that they can behave quite unpredictably. Most importantly of all, they cannot judge and assess danger in the way that adults with years of experience of traffic take for granted. Too many of our children are killed and injured because they simply don't know when they are in a dangerous situation. With this book parents and carers can help their children develop a sense of awareness, so they recognise potential dangers and know how to avoid them.

Of course all youngsters are individuals developing at different rates. Only the points of law referred to here are absolute rules. The other ideas and suggestions are offered as guides to introducing road safety to your children when you feel they're old enough to start learning the basic principles.

One of the best ways anyone can teach a child good road sense is by observing it themselves. Your own behaviour has a tremendous influence on your child's. For instance, if you make a point of crossing the road carefully, your child will learn to do the same. Many adults think that it is safe to skip in and out of traffic. It is not and it sets a bad example.

When you are out together, even when the child is very young, talk about what is happening around you. Draw attention to the changing colours of the traffic lights and how the cars stop when they are red or drive through when the lights are green. Explain why you choose to cross the road at a certain safe point; compare noises – the loud rumble of a heavy lorry to the almost silent swishing of a bicycle; play at spotting buses and motorcycles among the traffic; and, when the opportunity arises, grumble aloud about the anti-social or dangerous behaviour of road-users and explain why it is hazardous.

This may seem a bit much, particularly if your child is in a buggy or isn't yet talking fluently, but it's a fundamental part of developing good road sense. In drawing children's attention to what's going on around them, you are encouraging them to look and listen – and failure to look and listen are two of the particular causes of accidents among young road users.

By explaining to children as you cross roads or negotiate traffic hazards, you are actively demonstrating the kind of decisions that pedestrians constantly have to take; to stop, think, look and listen before acting. By the time the children are old enough to learn the Green Cross Code and begin to go out on their own, they will have absorbed a great deal of basic road sense.

If you're worried that your child may be picking up bad habits from other adults who take them out, talk to those adults about what you're trying to do. Suggest they read this book. Go out together so that you can demonstrate the routines you've established with the child. Explain that though they may seem time-consuming and even inconvenient, they are setting safe patterns for the child to follow. By dashing across a Pelican crossing while the little red man is showing, or squeezing through a gap between parked cars to cross the road, an unthinking adult can confuse a child and undo the good work.

Making children more alert to the hazards of traffic is one way of cutting the accident statistics. The other challenge is to teach adults to be more aware of the children in our streets. When you're driving, keep a special look-out for children. Don't assume that the child waiting to cross the road will automatically see or hear your vehicle coming, or wait for you to pass. You can make your own contribution to road safety by being extra vigilant as you pass schools, ice-cream vans, park entrances and other places popular with children. Even as a pedestrian you can keep an eye on the toddler whose father has let go of his hand for a few moments, or the child whose toy has fallen into the gutter and tries to go after it.

If all adults were to demonstrate just a little more concern and protection for children in the street, we might see child casualty statistics begin to fall.

Traffic

Small children may not understand what 'traffic' is and why it can be dangerous – so these issues are the first you should tackle when teaching road safety. Let's start with a simple naming exercise. Can your child identify these vehicles?

The next picture shows a busy street with vehicles in the road. Point to an identifiable object in the picture (it could be a vehicle, the policeman or the postbox) and ask what it is. When the child has identified it, ask if the object is 'traffic'. If the child is confused, explain that all vehicles are traffic; traffic travels along the road. The postbox is not traffic because it stands still on the pavement. Remember to point out that vehicles which are not moving can still be dangerous – they can become 'traffic' very suddenly!

Traffic, of whatever kind, is dangerous. Even a bicycle can injure a child who runs out in front of it. It's important to make this message clear to children in your care. Show them how big and heavy vehicles are. For example, stand by the road and feel the ground shake as a heavy lorry passes. Your aim isn't to terrify them but to impress on them the need for caution whenever there is traffic around. A child may learn to respect fire after burning his or her fingers on a match. A child who runs in front of a juggernaut may never have the opportunity to learn from the experience.

Here's Charlie with a lesson on size and weight.

- ● Which is the biggest?
- ● Which is the smallest?
- ● Which is the heaviest?
- ● Which is the lightest?

The following two pictures are for talking about with your child. Ask what's going on in them. Discuss what might happen next and what the dangers are. While you are doing this, stress the size and speed of the vehicles and the need to be very careful when there is traffic around.

Another important concept is 'hard' and 'soft'. Vehicles (on the outside) are 'hard'. People are 'soft'. 'Hard' vehicles hurt 'soft' people.

SPEED, DISTANCE AND SOUND

As adults we instinctively assess the speed and distance of approaching traffic. We take this ability so much for granted that it's sometimes difficult for us to appreciate that children don't have the same skills. Children simply don't see and hear things in the same way that adults do; their vision to the side is not well developed and they are less able to identify from which direction a sound is coming. Children have to learn to make judgements adults make instinctively.

To help them develop the critical skills they need to be safe in the streets, we can help develop the concepts of speed, distance and sound. These are the main factors we use when making the decision to cross a road.

SPEED.

Your child will already have some knowledge of speed, but try to apply that knowledge to situations involving traffic. Here are some activities you might try.

Stand at a set of traffic lights and watch the cars slow down for red lights and slowly pull away when the light changes to green. See how, on the green light, some cars drive through fast. Slow and fast are the key words. Ask your child to assess the speed of an approaching car. Is it slow or fast? Point out that some vehicles, such as milkfloats, always go very slowly, while others, such as sports cars, often go very fast.

- Who is going fast?
- Who is going slowly?

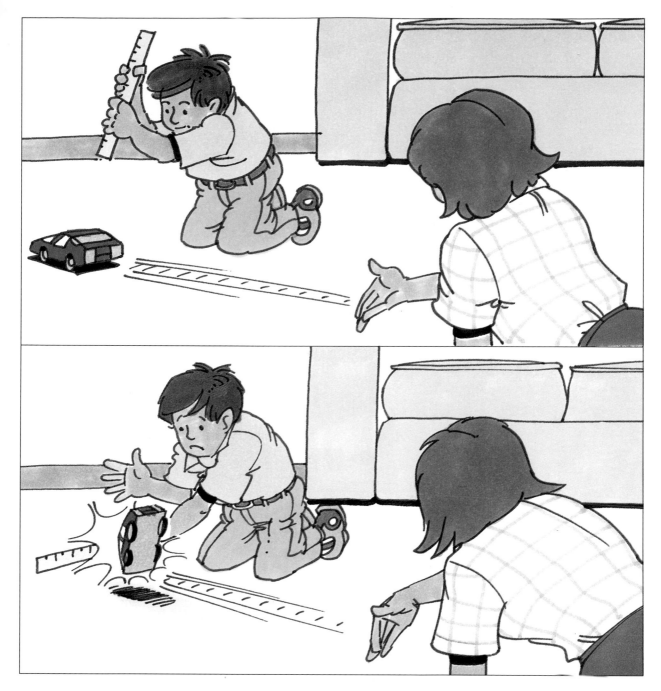

Toy cars can be useful when teaching about speed. Sit the child on the floor with a ruler or pencil. He or she holds the ruler on the floor while you push a toy car towards him or her. Sometimes you push it slowly, and the child has plenty of time to pull the ruler away. Sometimes you push it fast, so he or she has to act more quickly. Talk about what is happening as you play. When the car goes fast there's no time to get out of the way. If the car is going slowly there is plenty of time to move. Talk about how this also applies to real cars and pedestrians in the road.

DISTANCE.

Even small children will have a basic understanding of how distance affects what we see. To be safe in the street, they have to be able to apply this understanding to traffic.

There are dozens of games you and your child can play to learn about distance. Try standing on opposite sides of a room and gradually moving towards each other, keeping your eyes on each other's nose. (It will help if you get down on your knees!) End up rubbing noses – and see how huge noses look at this close range. Explain the principle; when things are far away they look small, but when they are close up they look big.

When you are waiting for a bus, practise spotting it some distance away. Draw the child's attention to the way in which it gradually grows in size as it approaches. You can use these pictures as a talking point.

Here's the bus! Is it far away or near?

Here's the bus! Is it far away or near?

Take your child to a long, stretch of road, preferably one without too much traffic. A footbridge over a main road is ideal if there is one near you. Practise spotting a tiny vehicle in the distance and following it with your eye and finger as it gradually looms larger.

Play a guessing game. When you first spot it, guess what kind of vehicle it is – big (i.e. lorry or coach), medium (i.e. van or minibus) or small (i.e. car or motorbike)? As it comes nearer you'll be able to see if you were right. Try Charlie's test.

16

- Which vehicle is far away?
  Which vehicle is near?
- Which vehicle looks the biggest
  from here?
- If the two vehicles were parked
  next to each other, which would
  be the biggest?
- Why does Charlie's head look
  bigger than the lorry?

SOUND.

Sound is the third major factor we use to make judgments in traffic. One of the easiest ways of demonstrating how distance affects sound is to go into the garden or park with your child and stand face to face. Start singing a favourite song and walk gradually away from each other until the sound becomes faint. Then walk back together again.

When you are out with your child you can play listening games. If you are walking along a very quiet road with little traffic, you can have a competition with the child to see who can hear something coming first. The first to shout 'Something's coming!' is the winner.

When children have got the hang of this game, encourage them to use sound to help them judge the speed of the vehicle. When you hear a noisy vehicle shout, 'Something might be coming fast!'

When your children play with toy cars, encourage them to make appropriate noises. Teach them to make a siren noise for a fire engine or ambulance, and explain that anything with a siren blaring is likely to be moving quickly.

When you are waiting for a bus you can play a game by asking children to shut their eyes (make sure you're holding hands firmly) and shout 'Now!' when they judge from the noise that a vehicle is passing by. They can then open their eyes and see if they were right. If a bicycle or any other vehicle glides past without being heard, point this out – because not all traffic makes a noise. Try Charlie's noise test and see how aware of traffic noise your child is already.

- Which vehicle is the noisiest?
- Which is the quietest?
- Which vehicle makes a tinkling noise as it goes along?

If children have a reasonable sense of traffic speed, distance and noise and understand the way these three factors are related, they will be equipped to begin to make the kind of judgements necessary when crossing the road. Here's a test to see whether your child has a grasp of the way speed, sound and distance are related. Discuss the picture and, if your child is still confused, explain the correct answers.

- If all three vehicles were parked next to each other, which would be the biggest?
- Which vehicle do you think might sound loudest?
- Which vehicle might be going the fastest?
- Which vehicle is far away from Charlie?
- Which vehicle is nearest Charlie?
- Which looks bigger – Charlie or the coach?
- Who is bigger – Charlie or the coach?

Remember, the most effective way of teaching children about traffic speed, distance and sound is to allow them to experience these things in safety. Whenever you are out together and a car flashes past or a lorry rumbles swiftly by, point it out to children and talk about speed, noise and distance. In this way you will make them alert to what is happening around them and develop their ability to assess the dangers for themselves.

In The Street

To an adult the distinction between the road and the pavement is obvious. Roads are for vehicles, pavements are for people. It's so simple we don't give it a second thought. Unfortunately it's not so obvious to small children, especially if they live in the country where there are no pavements, or a city where pavements are cluttered with parked cars.

Knowing the difference between the pavement and the road is very important. Unless children understand this, they won't be able to get to grips with crossing roads or walking safely in the street. How good is your child at distinguishing one from the other?

- Where is Charlie standing – on the pavement or in the road?

- Is Charlie on the pavement or the road?

If children have difficulty making the distinction between road and pavement, explain it to them when you look through picture books which show street scenes. When you are out together, draw attention to some of the other features of the street that we take for granted, such as pedestrian crossings and telephone boxes.

BUS STOP

LITTER BIN

Point to where each of these belongs. Is it on the road, or on the pavement?

THE KERB

It's important for children to understand that the kerb is the dividing line between the pavement and the road. **Near the kerb is the place where people stop before crossing the road.** Can your child recognise the kerb? Charlie wants to go home. Can you follow the kerb all the way to Charlie's House? Follow the kerb with your finger.

CHARLIE'S HOUSE

When you are out with children, try to make it a rule that they do not cross the kerb without checking with you that it's safe to do so. With time this will become an automatic reaction and they will be less likely to dash unthinkingly off the pavement. Try this test to see if your child is conscious of the need to stop at the kerb.

● In which picture should Charlie and his Mum stop?

To encourage this idea of stopping at the kerb, try practising it in a safe place well away from traffic. Find a convenient dividing line – between the patio and the lawn, for example – and agree with the children that one side is the road and the other the pavement. The children walk across the 'pavement' and you shout 'Stop!' just as they get to the 'kerb'. If they stop immediately and safely, swap places and they can instruct you. If they step over the 'kerb' into the 'road', get them to try again until they get it right.

TRAFFIC ON THE PAVEMENT

In urban areas it's common to see vehicles driving onto the pavement before parking. Vehicles also cross the pavement on driveways – and sometimes the driveways aren't easily distinguishable from the pavements themselves. When you are out with your child, point out any cars parked on the pavement and in driveways and explain that traffic doesn't always stay on the road – you have to watch out for traffic on the pavement as well. Can your child spot the dangers in these pictures? As you look at them together, ask what Charlie's doing wrong in each one and what he should do to be safe.

Charlie is in danger, shout 'Look out, Charlie!'.

Charlie is in danger, shout 'Look out, Charlie!'

Charlie is in danger, shout 'Look out, Charlie!'

ON COUNTRY ROADS

If you live in a rural area where there are no pavements, it's important to teach your children road sense by example. **No matter how quiet the road you're walking along, if at all possible keep to the right-hand side, facing any on-coming traffic. Keep to the side of the road and always walk between the child and the traffic.**

Though it's tempting to walk down the middle of a deserted lane, don't do it. Your adult senses may be alert to an approaching vehicle, but a child's attention is easily distracted. By walking down the middle of the road and behaving unguardedly, you're teaching children to take risks when they are out on their own.

These two pictures show the right way and the wrong way to walk in the country. Show your child which is which.

Charlie is not safe.

Charlie is safe.

Holding Hands

Holding hands is the most simple and fundamental rule of road safety. **Whenever you are out in the street or any place where your child could run into traffic danger – for example, at the entrance to your local park – hold the child's hand.** Children, not unnaturally, don't like being restrained in this way. Explain the need to hold hands by discussing the following four pictures with your child. They each show a danger that has arisen from not holding hands.

● What is happening in this picture?
Charlie is running into the road after the dog. He hasn't stopped to look at the traffic. He hasn't seen the car coming towards him.

● What is happening in this picture?
Charlie has tripped. He is falling over in the road. His Mum can't see what has happened.

● What is happening in this
   picture?
*Charlie is chasing his ball, which he
should not be playing with in the
street.*

● What is happening in this
   picture?
*Charlie is lost. He is very frightened.
He can't see his Mum.*

Holding hands is the safe and secure way of walking with a child in the street. But as every parent and carer knows, there are times when even the most careful adult has to let go for a few seconds to switch shopping bags round, find a tissue in a pocket or fold up the baby buggy. And it takes just a few seconds for a child to get into danger. If you are going out and know that you'll have your hands full, use reins or 'handcuffs' to restrain your child. Here's a picture for children to colour in. While they are colouring it, discuss the safety aspects with them.

- What's happening in this picture?
- What colour have you used for the safety reins?
- Do you hold hands when you go out?
- What is the child nearest the road doing wrong?
- What could happen next?

PAVEMENT BEHAVIOUR

If you've ever been tripped up by a small child cutting suddenly across the pavement into your path, you'll appreciate that it's never too early to teach some basic good manners. If you're holding a small child's hand he or she won't be able to get up to mischief, but don't allow any child in your care, whatever their age, to run riot on the pavement. Though it's fine to play observation games and talk as you're walking along, put your foot down about racing around, playing with a ball, skateboarding, rollerskating or generally messing about on pavements – particularly when they are crowded. It's rude and potentially dangerous behaviour.

Teach your child to give way to other pedestrians when necessary. The best way is by example. When you're out pushing the baby buggy or the shopping trolley show consideration to other pedestrians. Move out of the way if you see a wheelchair, an elderly person with a walking frame, or a blind person with a guide dog coming towards you.

Thank you, Charlie.

Your child's safety is down to you. If adults are thoughtful and careful whenever they go out, children will gradually learn to take care of themselves. **Encourage children to behave well whenever they are in the street. Teach them to treat traffic and other road users with the respect they deserve.**

See And Be Seen

Many road accidents occur for the simple reason that drivers and pedestrians fail to see each other properly. It's a problem that is particularly relevant to children who, being much smaller than adults, don't have a full range of vision and are less visible to traffic. Children are also at risk because their senses of sight and hearing are not as developed as adults'. Anything that impedes their vision or hearing while they are out in the street can be dangerous.

SEEING CLEARLY

To be safe on the roads we all have to be able to see clearly. You can help to protect your child by choosing clothing carefully, particularly winter gear such as parkas and anoraks. Many of these have hoods that come well over the face to give protection from the rain. But though they keep your child dry, they may also give tunnel vision.

The best solution to this problem is to make sure that hoods fit snugly around the face and don't act as blinkers. Check that when your children turn their heads, the hoods move with them and allow a clear view. As well as limiting the range of vision, hoods may also cut out noise. Not only can children not see the approaching traffic, but they are deaf to any warning noise.

Extra care is needed when children wearing hoods want to cross the road. The safest advice is to get them to put the hoods down so they can see and hear properly. It's better to have wet hair than a road accident.

Other hazards affecting vision include umbrellas. In driving rain it's tempting to lower the umbrella for protection as you wait at the kerb to cross the road with your child. If your children have umbrellas of their own they may copy you and stroll into the road without looking. Keep your umbrella raised above your head and set them a good example.

If children have personal stereos, ensure that they don't use them in the street when their ears should be concentrating on traffic noise, not the latest chart hit.

Here are five children with a test for you.

- Who can see clearly?
- Who can hear clearly?
- Who can see and hear clearly?

BE SEEN

Young children need to be easily seen by other road users. Dress your child in brightly-coloured clothing whenever possible and also use safety items like belts, sashes and arm bands which make them 'shine' day or night.

In poor daylight and dusk you'll need *fluorescent* items in yellow or lime green. Night-time calls for *reflective* items which reflect light right back to drivers or other road users. The best solution is to use items which combine both fluorescent and reflective materials.

● Charlie is out on a dark afternoon. What is he wearing? *Charlie is wearing dark clothing which cannot be easily seen. Now turn the page to find out what Charlie should be wearing.*

● What is Charlie wearing?
Charlie is wearing a Sam Browne belt, arm bands, a patch on his satchel, and leggings.

Bags and satchels can be decorated with fluorescent tape for daytime and reflective tape for night-time. You and your child can have a busy afternoon adding warning stripes and triangles to lunch-boxes, bags and accessories. You can add fluorescent and reflective flashes to the baby's buggy and your shopping bag.

PAINT

GLUE

Crossing The Road

Young children – normally those aged seven or under – should never go out or cross the road by themselves. Most children under seven cannot judge speed or distance accurately and they get easily distracted by things happening around them. You can start teaching your children the Green Cross Code at an earlier age, but don't allow them to cross roads alone until they are much older. When they cross the road with you, remember always to hold hands.

The full Green Cross Code is too much for small children to take in, but you can begin to teach the basics of road safety very early. Start with three simple steps, which you can teach children as you cross the road together:

STOP
Teach them to stop in a safe place on the pavement well away from the kerb.

LOOK
Look all round for traffic. Is it far away or near? Is it coming fast or slowly? What kind of traffic is it? Ideally, if there is any traffic do not try to cross.

LISTEN AND THINK
Can you hear any traffic coming? Is the noise loud or quiet? Before you do anything, think hard about what you can see and hear. Ask the children whether they think it is safe to cross. If they do, and it is safe, cross the road together, holding hands. If it is not safe, explain why.

Charlie is still too young to learn the full Green Cross Code but his older sister, Jo, has mastered the early steps. She has developed a reasonable degree of road sense and has started using the Green Cross Code to cross the road on her own.

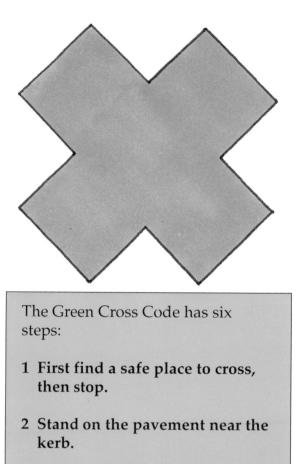

The Green Cross Code has six steps:

1 **First find a safe place to cross, then stop.**

2 **Stand on the pavement near the kerb.**

3 **Look all round for traffic and listen.**

4 **If traffic is coming, let it pass. Look all round again.**

5 **When there is no traffic near, walk straight across the road.**

6 **Keep looking and listening for traffic while you cross.**

Remember, the best way to teach is by example. So learn the code yourself, follow it and ask your child to participate with you in making decisions about where, when and how to cross the road. Before long the child will have learned not only the rules, but what they mean in practice.

41

1 First find a safe place to cross, then stop.

It's very important to find a safe spot to cross the road. Good places for children are Pelican crossings, Zebra crossings, traffic islands, footbridges, subways or places where there is a policeman, a 'lollipop' person or a traffic warden.

Teach your children not to stand between parked cars or on sharp bends before crossing. If there are no obviously safe crossing points, encourage them to look for an open space at a point where they can see the road clearly in both directions, and where drivers can see them.

- Can you see four places where it would be safe to cross the road?
- Can you see two people who will help you cross the road?
- Can you see any places where it would be dangerous to cross the road?

The four safe places to cross are: the footbridge, the Zebra crossing, the Pelican crossing and the subway.
The policeman and the lollipop person will help you cross the road.
Everywhere else should be considered dangerous to cross the road.

2 Stand on the pavement near the kerb.

Don't stand too near the edge of the pavement. Stop a little way back from the kerb – where you're safely away from the traffic but still able to see if anything is coming. If there is no pavement, stand back from the edge of the road but in a place where you can still see traffic coming.

3 Look all round for traffic and listen.
Traffic may be coming from all directions, so take care to look along every road nearby. And listen, too, because you can sometimes hear traffic before you can see it.

- Can you see all the places where traffic is coming from?
- Is there a safer place for Jo to cross?

The Pelican crossing would be a safer place for Jo to cross.

4 If traffic is coming, let it pass. Look all round again.

If there's any traffic near, let it pass. Then look around again and listen to make sure no more traffic is coming.

● Is there any traffic coming?

5 When there is no traffic near, walk straight across the road.

When there is no traffic near it's safe to cross. If there is something in the distance do not cross unless you are certain there's plenty of time.

Remember, even if traffic seems a long way off, it may be coming very fast. When you're sure it's safe, walk straight across the road – don't run.

● Is it safe for Jo to cross the road?

6 Keep looking and listening for traffic while you cross.

Once you're in the road, keep looking and listening in case some traffic appears.

● Can you see a car coming?

DANGER SPOTS

Accident statistics show that there are certain spots and occasions when children are in particular danger while crossing roads. Here are three illustrated examples. Discuss them with your child and explain why they are so dangerous.

Crossing between parked cars.
Children are smaller than adults. If they stand between parked cars while trying to cross the road, they not only find it difficult to see and hear traffic approaching, but they are hidden from the view of drivers. **If you have to cross where there are parked cars choose your place very carefully and use the Green Cross Code from the outer edge of the parked cars.**

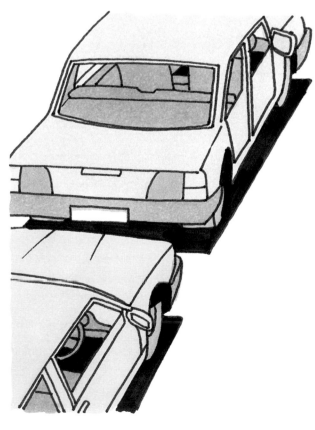

Crossing in front of a bus. Getting off a bus and then walking in front of it to cross the road involves an immense risk to adults and children alike. It's not only difficult to see any traffic coming round the bus, but it's also extremely difficult for the driver to see anyone standing directly in front of the vehicle. Train your children to wait on the pavement until the bus has gone and then cross the road.

Crossing near ice-cream vans. The chimes of an ice-cream van are enough to make even the most sensible children forget all the road safety rules they've ever learned. When you hear the chimes or see a parked ice-cream van, remind your children to be careful and hold their hands. Once they've bought ice-creams, older children should cross the road behind the van, not in front of it.

USING CROSSINGS

Pelican and Zebra crossings are only safe if your child knows how to use them properly.

At a Pelican crossing, if the red man signal shows press the button and wait. When the green man signal appears and all vehicles have stopped moving, walk carefully across the road. After a short while the green man symbol will start to flash. You should not start to cross the road when the signal is flashing because this means that the light is about to change to red. If the green man starts to flash while you are crossing, don't worry – you'll have time to get to the other side.

● Should Jo cross the road now?
Yes – the green man signal is showing. Cross carefully.

● Should Jo cross the road now?
No – the red man signal is showing. Wait.

● Should Jo cross the road now?
Jo should not start to cross when the green man symbol is flashing.

At a Zebra crossing, stand close to the kerb so that drivers can see that you definitely want to cross the road. Give drivers plenty of time to slow down and stop for you. Remember, not all drivers will automatically stop for you. When the traffic on both sides of the road has stopped, walk carefully across the road.

● Is it safe for Jo to cross the road now?
No she must wait until all vehicles have stopped.

On the next page you'll find a game to play. It's called THE CROSSING GAME and it's designed to make children think about crossing the road in safety. To play THE CROSSING GAME:

1 Turn to pages 62 and 63. You'll see 16 cards with pictures of four kites, four apples, four hats and four badges. There are also four figures and two dice. Cut out all the pieces and assemble them as shown.

2 THE CROSSING GAME can be played by up to four people. Each player chooses a figure and puts it on one of the START squares – there are four around the board. The youngest player has first throw of the dice, the oldest is last to throw.

3 The aim of the game is to cross the road and get one of the ice-creams – you can see the ice-cream stall in the centre of the board. But before you can have an ice-cream, you must collect an apple, a kite, a hat and a badge from the four stalls around the board.

4 To start, throw the dice with the numbers. Move your figure the correct number of squares along the pavement in any direction. You should aim to land on one of the FREE GIFT squares. If you do, take a card that matches the free gift.

5 When you have collected a free gift, you have to cross the road to the next section of the board to collect your next free gift. Throw the numbered dice and move your figure until you land exactly on one of the crossing points.

6 If you've reached a Zebra crossing, miss one go, then cross the road to the other side. If it's a Pelican crossing, throw the other dice; you need to throw the green man symbol before you can cross. If you get any other symbol you have to wait for your next turn and try again. If you're waiting at the school crossing patrol, throw the dice; you need to score a yellow lollipop person before you can safely cross. If you throw any other symbol, you must wait until your next turn and try again.

7 When you have visited all four stalls and claimed your four free gifts, cross the road to the ice-cream stall. The first person to get there is the winner.

PEOPLE TO CROSS THE ROAD WITH

As a parent or carer, you will almost certainly have warned your child of the dangers of talking to strangers in the street. According to the classic advice, if they need assistance to cross the road they can safely rely on a policeman, a school crossing patrol or a traffic warden to help. This is fine as far as it goes, but in real life policemen, traffic wardens and lollipop patrols are

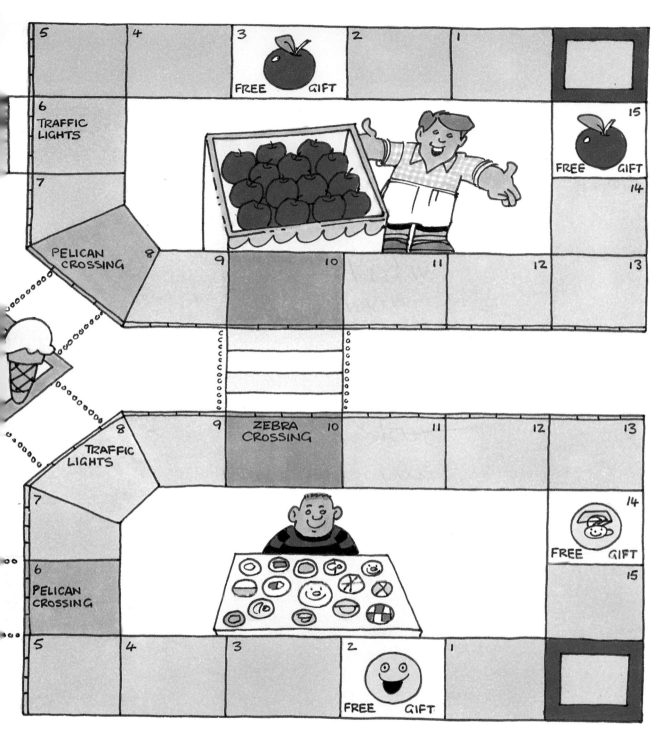

thin on the ground when they are most needed – in fact your child could come to harm while waiting for one to appear.

The only answer to this difficult situation is to make sure that it doesn't happen. The best way of protecting your child is to ensure that he or she never has to decide between risking a nervous dash across a busy street or asking a stranger for help.

Playing Safe

For the under fives, the only safe places to play are securely fenced-in gardens and back yards, parks and playgrounds. Even in these safe areas, children shouldn't be left unsupervised.

Even if you live in a quiet street, don't allow your child to play in the road. By allowing kids to kick a ball around or ride their tricycles in the road, or on the pavement you encourage them to feel at ease there. For their own safety they need to be on guard whenever they are near a road. Sooner or later, no matter how deserted your cul-de-sac, a lost driver will choose it as the ideal place to do a quick turn – and your unwary child may be in the way.

Teach your children that footpaths, pavements and grass verges are not playgrounds. Children on skateboards, roller-skates, go-karts or playing games are not only a nuisance to pedestrians but potentially dangerous, too. It takes only a split second for them to lose control and career in front of a car.

Don't encourage your child to play in the driveway or anywhere near cars – not even your own family car. Every year children are injured after being reversed into by drivers who didn't see them playing quietly behind the parked car.

Remember to keep garden gates shut at all times. Install bolts or fastenings out of children's reach, so they can't let themselves out when you're not looking. Ask the milkman and the postman to shut the front gate behind them every day, or better still adapt it so that it swings shut automatically. When you open your front door, you don't want your toddler to make a dash down the garden path and straight into the path of an on-coming car.

When you're taking children to the park or playground, carry your footballs, skateboards, tricycles, tennis rackets and other play equipment with you – don't play with them on the pavement. Even something as harmless as a tennis ball can cause an accident if it flies into the windscreen of an unsuspecting driver. Here's a picture to discuss with your child while he or she colours it in.

Children As Passengers

SEAT BELTS AND CHILD RESTRAINTS

Around the country, 7,000 children are injured or killed each year because they are not properly restrained while travelling in cars. You don't have to be speeding or driving dangerously to kill your child in your own car. If you hit something at just 30 m.p.h., children like Charlie and Jo sitting unrestrained in the rear seat can fly forward through the windscreen. In just one fifth of a second their skulls can be fractured and their faces torn to shreds. This kind of tragedy happens every day.

You can prevent it happening to you by ensuring that your child – and other people's children who travel with you use correctly fitted safety restraints approved for their size and weight. As the *Highway Code* says, 'If you are involved in an accident, wearing a seat belt halves the risk of death or serious injury.'

THE LAW

All drivers and passengers must wear a seat belt, unless exempt for medical or other legally specified reasons. Children under twelve months must be in an approved child restraint designed for infants of their weight and size. Children over one year are legally required to wear an adult seat belt, which for obvious safety reasons should be used in conjunction with an approved child seat or booster cushion.

In the rear seat

Any child under the age of fourteen travelling in the back of a car that has rear seat belts or other restraints must use them, unless there is a special reason for not doing so. These reasons might include the fact that the seats and seat belts are being used by adults, or that the seat belts are being used to secure a carrycot containing a baby. If this situation occurs often, fit lap belts or some other kind of restraint for the child.

As a general rule, it is better for a child to sit in the front of the car in a special child seat or using a booster cushion and adult seatbelt than to travel unrestrained in the back.

Here are two families going out in the car. You'll recognise Charlie and Jo's family, they always use seat belts and restraints. The other family, the Riskys, don't bother. Let your child spot some of the dangers and safety points in the pictures.

- Which car belongs to Charlie's family?
- Which car belongs to the Risky family?
- How many dangers can you spot in the Risky's car?
- How many dangers can you spot in Charlie's family's car?

CHOOSING SAFETY RESTRAINTS

Choose restraints that meet the British Safety Standard; they will carry the kitemark symbol that assures you of their quality. Check that your purchase is suitable for your make of car – some types of child seat are more difficult to secure in certain models. Read the fitting instructions carefully and carry them out. If you are given or lent child seats and booster cushions that don't carry the kitemark and don't seem adequate for the purpose, forget them and buy reliable replacements.

For babies from birth to nine months old specially designed infant carriers should be used. In most of them, the children face backwards and are held securely in a harness so that even if the car overturns they are protected. These infant carriers also occupy only one seat.

From the age of nine months to four years, children should travel in approved child seats. These hold them securely and give much greater protection than booster cushions and seat belts. It's easy for a small child to slide out of a seat belt, even while sitting on a booster cushion.

Child safety harnesses or booster cushions are suitable for children from four upwards. Booster cushions raise children so that they can safely and comfortably wear the standard adult seat belts fitted in all recent cars. They are held in place by straps and fixings which keep them steady and prevent children sliding out in the event of an accident. There is no substitute for a well-designed booster cushion. Don't prop children up on household cushions; if these slide away from beneath the children could slip out of the seat belts or even be throttled by them. Here's Charlie with another test for you:

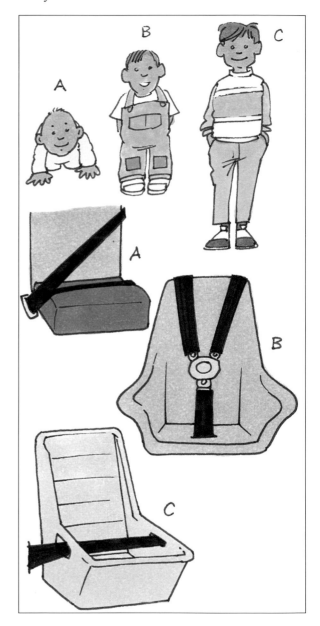

● Who should sit in each seat?
Child A should sit in the infant carrier (C).
Child B should sit in the child seat (B).
Child C should use the booster cushion and adult seat belt (A).

ON HOLIDAY

If you are going to hire a car either in this country or abroad, check with the hire company that infant carriers, child seats and booster cushions can be supplied, and that they are of an adequate standard. It may be necessary to reserve them in advance. If you have problems with smaller companies, invest in your childrens' safety and use one of the bigger (and more expensive) multinational hire companies, who can offer a better range of safety equipment. Your child's safety has to be worth more than a few extra pounds.

When you're going on holiday, don't load the car with so much luggage that children's safety seats have to be left at home. It's better to use a roof rack or tow a trailer with luggage than to have the children bouncing around unrestrained along with the suitcases and buckets and spades.

OTHER PEOPLE'S CARS

People without children – and even those with them – may not have safety seats and booster cushions in their cars. If you think it's unsafe for your child to travel in a friend's car, and you can't transfer your own seats and boosters to the other car, refuse the lift and transport your child yourself. Be equally firm when transporting other people's children; carry only as many as you can in safety – don't cram them into the back seat and hope for the best.

Almost inevitably there will come a day when children have to ride unrestrained in the back seat of a car. You can make them as safe as possible in this situation by teaching them not to stand up between the front seats, or stand or kneel in the gap between front

and rear seats. If you are with them, wear a seatbelt and hold them firmly on your lap in the rear seats, not in the front seat. If they are large enough to use an adult seat belt, the law requires them to be strapped in – even if it means they can't see out of the window.

Teach children always to get out of the side of the car nearest the pavement. They should never get out into the road.

If your child has to travel alone in a taxi – to school, for example – arrange for the taxi to come equipped with a booster cushion and seat belt or some other kind of safety harness. If the taxi isn't equipped in this way (and many are not) and if the rear seats are not separated from the driver by a partition protest to your local authority.

● Why is this child not safe? What would happen if there was an accident?

● Is this child safe? What would happen if there was an accident?

● What has Dad Risky done wrong? What would be safer?

PUBLIC TRANSPORT

Teach your children to behave properly when they use buses and coaches. Make it clear, from an early age, that buses are not places for play. Be firm with your children; don't allow them to rush up and down the aisle, clamber up and down the stairs or dangle from the handrails.

Whenever you wait for a bus, set your child a good example by queuing calmly and waiting your turn to get on. Let other people off the bus first. Above all, if you need to cross the road after getting off a bus, don't walk in front of it while it's still standing at the stop. Wait for it to pull away, then cross.

● What would happen to this child if the bus stopped suddenly?

ON JOURNEYS

If you're going on a long journey in the car or by public transport, keep children occupied. Take books, pencils, paper and story tapes which they can listen to on the car stereo or on a personal stereo. You can play pencil and paper games like noughts and crosses, or observation games like I-Spy. If you're off the motorway you can play Legs, a game in which you have to add up the number of legs that appear on the pub signs you pass – so the Red Lion has four legs, the Fox and Goose six legs and the Horse and Hounds ... lots of legs!

Journeys are also excellent times for developing a child's observation skills. Give children a short list of relatively common sights to spot – a church steeple, a black and white cow, a woman wearing red trousers, an Alsatian dog, for example – and see who can collect them first.

Car journeys also offer a good opportunity for teaching your children about road signs and road sense. Ask them to read the road signs as you travel along and tell you what they mean and what, if anything, you should do in response to them. They'll need help to begin with, so make sure you know the answers yourself. For less than £1 you can buy a copy of the *Highway Code.* Once you've read it and refreshed your memory, keep it in the car glove compartment for reference.

To see how much your children already know about road signs and their meaning, Charlie's here with a quiz. All you have to do is pair up the road sign with the correct message.

ROAD WORKS

ROUNDABOUT

TURN LEFT

PEDESTRIAN CROSSING

NO OVERTAKING

TWO-WAY TRAFFIC STRAIGHT AHEAD

NO CYCLING

SLIPPERY ROAD

Here's another road sign quiz. Can your children guess what these signs mean? Where would they expect to see them? For example, you might expect to see the low-flying aircraft sign near an airport. Use your copy of the *Highway Code* to find out the other answers!

ADULT BEHAVIOUR

Road sense can't be learned from a book. Children need to experience traffic themselves, in the safe company of a knowledgeable, responsible adult. If you're alert and careful when you are out in traffic with them, they'll learn to be alert and careful too. If you discuss and explain the things you see and do together, they'll have good practical experience on which to base their own judgements.

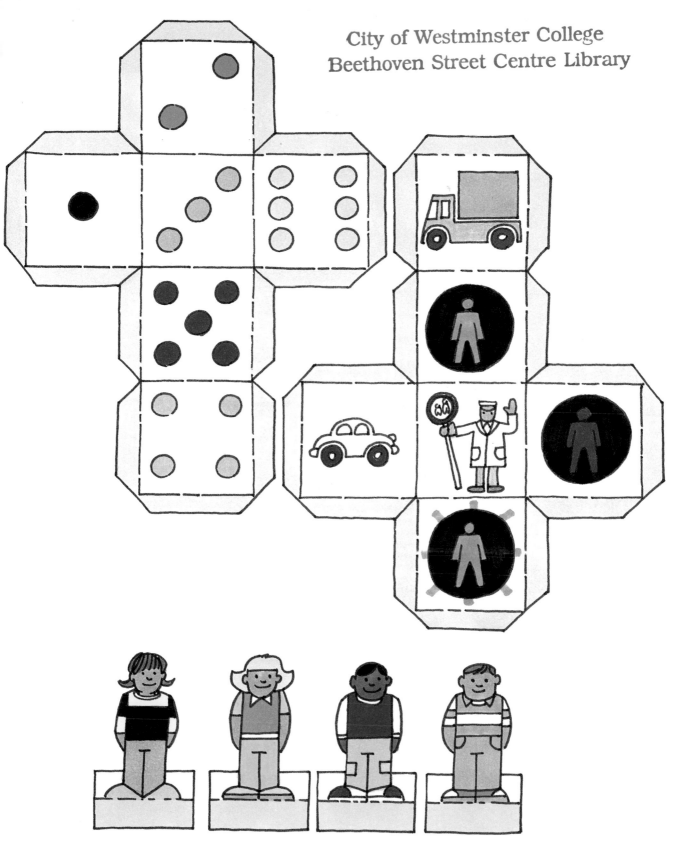

63

Printed in the UK for HMSO
Dd. 294375 C 200 11/91